## Other Works by This Author

*Spirits Speak*

*You Bet Your Life After Death*

*The Moment of Death*

*The 5$^{th}$ Secret*

*The 4 Secrets of the Universe*

*All About the Soul's Journey*

*The Book of Manifesting*

*Mysteries, Prophecies, and the Hollow Earth*

*The Lightness of Being*

*Sojourn*

*Poet Gone Wild*

*Poems of Life, Love, and the Meaning of Meaning*


### ***Infinite Healing***

*Poems and Messages for the
Loss of a Loved One*

*Poems and Messages for the
Loss of Your Animal Companion*

# WE'RE OFF TO SEE THE WIZARD

Spirit Messages from the Cast and Creators
of *The Wizard of Oz* ...and Toto, too

## PAUL GORMAN

Copyright © 2025 Paul J. Gorman
All Rights Reserved

Year of the Book
135 Glen Avenue
Glen Rock, PA 17327

ISBN: 978-1-64649-531-3 (paperback)
ISBN: 978-1-64649-532-0 (ebook)

Cover photo licensed from Alamy.
Other images in the public domain.

No part of this publication may be reproduced, distributed, or transmitted in any form or by any means, including photocopying, recording, or other electronic or mechanical methods, without the prior written permission of the author, except in the case of brief quotations embodied in critical reviews and certain other noncommercial uses permitted by copyright law.

## Contents

Foreword ................................................................. 1
Judy Garland – Dorothy ......................................... 2
Terry – Toto ............................................................ 5
Margaret Hamilton – Miss Gulch/Wicked Witch ... 6
Ray Bolger – Hunk/Scarecrow ............................... 9
Jack Haley – Hickory/Tin Woodsman .................. 13
Bert Lahr – Zeke/Cowardly Lion ......................... 16
Frank Morgan – Professor Marvel/etc. ................ 19
Victor Fleming – Director ..................................... 22
King Vidor – Director ........................................... 26
Billie Burke – Glinda ............................................ 29
Charley Grapewin – Uncle Henry ........................ 33
Clara Blandick – Auntie Em ................................. 36
Pat Walshe – Nikko ............................................... 39
L. Frank Baum – Author ....................................... 42
Appendix – Biographies ....................................... 45
About the Author .................................................. 49

## Foreword

This is a book of channeled messages from the spirits of the primary cast and creators of the 1939 movie, *The Wizard of Oz*.

**Question to Judy Garland – can you please help me come up with a title for this book?**
**It will be all spirit messages from the people who created *The Wizard of Oz* movie.**
**I have already considered:**

> 'Somewhere Over the Rainbow'

> 'Toto, I Have a Feeling We're Not in Kansas Anymore'

> 'There's No Place Like Home'

**What do you suggest?**
*'We're Off to See the Wizard'*

**I love it!**
*I could have made it, 'Ding Dong, the Cast is Dead – Not Just the Witch'.*

## Judy Garland – Dorothy

**Can I speak with Judy Garland?**
*I am delighted I can be heard by Gorman in his mind.*

**Hello, Judy. I am writing another book about the moment of death. Can you please tell me what your experience was like?**
**I am sorry that you died at the young age of 47, and I really enjoyed your singing – especially in *The Wizard of Oz* movie.**
*I died from having too many anti-depressants in one night. What I needed had nothing to do with taking pills.*

*I needed a lot of love, and it had to come from inside of me, having no other place it could come from.*

**Did you know you had died at first?**
*I knew, and it didn't matter in my logic. I lived in the limelight, and would have traded it for love any day.*

**Did angels meet you?**
*I had been met in my mind by angels, and also a guide advisor who had always been with me.*

*He – if he had a gender – helped me throughout my life.*

*"Am I really dead?" is what I said to them, and they all said it was my choice if I wanted it.*

**I imagine it was like when you were Dorothy in *The Wizard of Oz*. The Good Witch Glinda said all you have to do is click your heels together 3 times, and say, "There's no place like home."**
*I had not considered it like that, but it was a lot like that scene.*

**Please tell me about your experience.**
*A guide, and my angels – of which there were four – all came into my head like it was a meeting about how I could live or die in the next moment, if I chose that option. Needless to say, I had decided I did not want to live any longer.*

*I was in a delightful, blissful world of lightness and lovingness.*

*As soon as I made my decision known, I had the most intense light in my head that pulled me into it all the way, from my head.*

**Then what happened?**
*I had died at that moment, and it was exhilarating, to say the least. I was God in that moment – all lovingness, and all peacefulness. "In that moment" is in all moments, because all in God is one instant.*

**Thank you, Judy. Would you like to add anything else?**
*I illuminate in love now. Be love, and illuminate God in life.*

## Terry – Toto

**'Toto' was a female Cairn Terrier, originally named 'Terry'. She lived from 1933 to 1945, and appeared in 17 films, including *The Wizard of Oz*.**
**May I speak with Toto?**

*I am a little dog named, 'Toto', or 'Terry'. I lived an entirely different life than most dogs and animals. I had a job, and I did the best that I could.*

*I live in a Light Body, and a Light Mind now, and I can hear how I am loved in my movie parts.*

*All I can hear in your mind is if I loved my life in Hollywood. I did love my life, and I cannot have anything but love for my life – in my earthly life, and in my spirit life.*

*I am a guide in having my lifetime movie parts heal in peoples' minds, allowing them to laugh at my antics. All of their laughter heals me in my spiritual home.*

**Thank you, Toto.**
*Call me if I can be of any guidance from my home in the Mind of God.*

## Margaret Hamilton –
## Miss Gulch/Wicked Witch

**Margaret Hamilton died in 1985, at the age of 82, six months after entering a nursing home in Connecticut.**
**May I speak with Margaret?**
*I can hear if I am going to be an Almira Gulch character in this communication.*

*I had not had it in mind, but I could be another character having only love in my energy heart and mind. I couldn't be anything else, anyhow.*

**You are best known for your Almira Gulch/Wicked Witch of the West character in the 1939 movie, *The Wizard of Oz*.**
*I am, but I had a lot more to offer as an educator of young minds.*

**I am writing another book about life after death. What can you tell me about that?**
*It has a lot of similarities to 'The Wizard of Oz', as I heard in your mind. I had not considered it like that, but now I know that it does.*

*All Dorothy had to do was decide she was going home, and a Good Witch allowed her entry into a land of her soul family. Death is almost the same thing, having an angel instead of a Good Witch.*

*All I can do is have healing thoughts, which is like Dorothy exclaiming how beautiful it was in her dream. In her advanced awareness, she had moments of introspection with her mind, her heart, and her courage. It is amazing in its analogous meaning.*

*Not healing moves her into another dream with her mind, her heart, and her courage.*

*In it, she can become confused by attacks from her ego demands, or flying monkeys in this film analogy. Her insistence on being lost is what keeps her lost, for her entire dream.*

*Almira, as the Witch, is the one who tipped her off to having her own personal power.*

*Her angel, or Good Witch, advised her not to give it away.*

*It is an excellent analogy for living in a dream.*

**Thank you, Margaret.**
*I no longer have an hourglass, because I am in timelessness – but in a dream, it can be as long as it has a purpose for healing your mind.*

**How would you recommend for us to heal our minds?**
*Imagine all of your life has been a dream, and dreaming has its advantages because it can be anything you imagine it could be.*

*"All I have is my power, and my angelic guidance. I direct my mind, my heart, and my courage to hear them only."*

*Affirming it makes it heal in your mind, which is having a dream.*

**Thank you, Margaret.**
*I am grateful for having this communication.*

## Ray Bolger – Hunk/Scarecrow

**Ray Bolger died of bladder cancer in a nursing home, in 1987, at the age of 83.**
**May I speak with Ray?**
*I am allowing my heart and mind to have the courage in hearing Mr. Gorman's communication –having a degree in 'Thinkology', you know.*

**You were the best 'Scarecrow', Ray! It seems everyone was perfectly cast in the 1939 *The Wizard of Oz* movie, but you were originally cast as the 'Tin Woodsman'.**
*I am a dancer, not a mechanical man. I mean, I could not have been more poorly cast for being a Tin Woodsman.*

**You were an incredible dancer. There are videos online of you dancing in the 1930's.**
*Actually, I had a lot of hard times in doing some of those dance moves.*

**They looked impossible – especially the 180-degree splits, where you then hiked yourself straight up a few times. The performances took incredible strength and agility.**
*All could have been a lot harder if I wasn't working on them all the time.*

**What would you like to say about *The Wizard of Oz* story?**

*It always had a lot of meaning for me, because I loved everyone I worked with in making the film, although I could not hear in my costume headgear very well.*

### If you represented Dorothy's mind, what did the Wicked Witch represent?
*It had to be her fears of death, and losing her dog and family members.*

### That's a great answer. What do you think the Wizard represented?
*The all-powerful Wizard had to be her imagining there could be another being having power over her life – even the fraudster character who could not help her in her despair.*

### Ray, can you tell me what happened at the time of your death?
*I had a lot of pain in my bladder, not knowing it was cancer. Bladder pain is merciless in its debilitation. I had gotten a lot of medications, but nothing helped me to heal.*

*How come I got bladder cancer – I hear in your mind? I created it in controlling myself, by having incontinence – meaning no more control.*

*Incontinent means inconvenient.*

### Were you met by angels before you died?
*I had been met in my dreams, and in my mind. Having no hope for healing my cancer, all of my angelic visitors counseled me on leaving my body behind. They all made it sound more appealing to leave my body.*

*One day, an angel asked me if I was going home, and I asked it, "How can I go home if I am cancer-ridden?" A light explosion hit me in the head, and I got the angel's message. I had gone home instantly.*

*How could I have been healed, and gone home –without leaving my body – I hear in your mind? I could have, if I had enough insight to heal my mind of its need for controlling my body. I needed the discipline for my dancing routines, when I had been dancing in my earlier years.*

**What happened after that?**
*Angels, and a few people I had known, came into my mind, and gave me a big welcome home party – like I had been gone for a long time.*

*Here is a little-known fact – I had never left. I forgot that I left, and like in 'The Wizard of Oz' movie, I had to find my way back.*

*I can hear in your mind, asking if I am in communication with Judy, and other members of the movie troupe. I am, and all have one healing message for everyone who is reading this – "Love is only in all that you have love for –it is the only place it can be."*

**That's perfect – thank you, Ray.**

*It is perfect – have it heal in your mind by loving all in your life, all of the time.*

*The time isn't real – only the love.*

## JACK HALEY – HICKORY/TIN WOODSMAN

**Jack Haley died of a heart attack in 1979, at the age of 81.**
**May I speak with Jack?**
*All I can hear is if I had my heart attack because my heart had been broken.*

*I did, making me have one that is not breakable now.*

**Was life heartbreaking?**
*It is all about heartbreak, in my opinion. All heartbreak has one thing in common – it hurts having love in your heart, that cannot be loved in return.*

*Nothing in life is guaranteed, except that God will heal your heart. I had mine healed – it is as good as new – even better because it has no love limits, and it cannot be broken.*

**Can you please tell me what happened when you died?**
*I had a lot of heat in my head, and pain in my chest. All I could think was, "I'm not having a heart attack, I'm not having a heart attack." I did have a heart attack. I died immediately, and my body died shortly after that.*

*In my 'all awareness, healed in the light' stage, I could not have felt better. I still do, although I am one moment in God always, meaning eternally. I can allow this communication, and anything else I can heal my soul in.*

**Did an angel meet you when you had a heart attack?**
*An angel did meet me in my mind, giving me options. One option it gave me had nothing in it I was interested in. It said I could live, if I needed more earthly time, but I felt so good, I didn't need anything on the Earth.*

*The next option it gave me asked me if I could imagine God and myself being one.*

*I answered with, "No, I can't."*

*Incredibly, I became God – and have not been able to see myself as not-God again.*

*I am you, and you are God also. You just don't have my God-awareness testimonial.*

**You received "a testimonial" from the Wizard, in *The Wizard of Oz* movie.**
*All we had been given is what we already had. We did not know it had been there all along. That is how art imitates life. The movie characters looked for one thing they didn't believe they had in themselves – and looked outside of themselves for it to be given to them. In the end, it became clear they all possessed the qualities they had been looking for.*

*How could life be any other way? That is what life is for.*

**That's beautiful. Thank you, Jack.**

I am all aware, and now healed from this Gorman communication.

**Do aspects of God need to heal?**
*Not heal, but become one with God in one moment for me – and in all moments for you.*

## BERT LAHR – ZEKE/COWARDLY LION

**Bert Lahr died in 1967, at the age of 72. He was hospitalized for back pain, and it was reported that he died of pneumonia. His son said he succumbed to cancer, and the official cause of death was "massive intestinal hemorrhage." May I speak with Bert?**

*Aw shucks, I am in a Gorman communication. I am Bert – hello, Mr. Gorman.*

**Hello, Bert. Before we talk about life and your after-life, what happened at the time of your death?**

*All cancers have one thing in common – they grow until they can't grow anymore.*

*How could I have had cancer growing in my gut, and not been aware of it, I hear you asking?*

*I did have a feeling I may have cancer, but I decided I could live a normal life if I did not get cancer treatments that would have ended my life before the cancer did.*

**That is still largely true today, almost 60 years later.**

*All I can add is that cancer is more widespread and aggressive than in my lifetime.*

**What happened when you died?**

*I had an incredibly bright light come into my hospital room, and I had a good feeling when it was there.*

*It communicated with me in my mind, about how I could have all I ever desired, if I asked for it.*

*Of course, I loved hearing that. All I had to do was ask for anything, and allow it – and God would give it to me.*

*I needed my courage again, because I did not imagine that dying could be so beautiful, for me anyway.*

*It gave me all courage, love, and peace – wrapped in all awareness.*

*God gave it to me, meaning I gave it to myself.*

**Since you died, the importance and popularity of *The Wizard of Oz* movie has grown exponentially, and it is considered one of the best movies ever made.**
*It has humanity meeting inhumanity in the mean Witch character.*

*All of the characters had been invited into Dorothy's dream, and all had been included in it for her to heal them.*

**Thank you very much, Bert.**
*Courage has been given to all of life, making it your God-given nature.*

*Allow it entry into each of your thoughts and words.*

## Frank Morgan – Professor Marvel/Doorman/Cabbie/Guard/Wizard

**Frank Morgan died of a heart attack in 1949, at the age of 59. He was found dead in bed.
May I speak with Frank?**
*I am Frank – how may I be of assistance to you?*

*I already know how I can be of assistance, don't I?*

*Allow me to detail my adventures of chasing away death, and defeating almost impossible odds of ever making it to heaven – but I made it, and despite my treacherous journey, I am here to tell the tale.*

**Thank you, Professor Marvel!**
*I am not a marvel, you can be sure of that – but I have one thing that is marvelous.*

*I am God, having a dream that I am you – and you have figured out that I am you having a dream.*

**Can you tell me what happened when you died?**
*I died in my bed. If I had to choose a place, that was it. How could I choose a place?*

*"Leave that to me," is what I always said. Life is all about having a choice – and choices are healing, or hurting in each moment.*

*How could I choose my location at the time of my death?*

*I chose it before I was born, having decided I was going to die in my bed, in my sleep.*

*Is there a better choice?*

**You are right, that is the best choice. Did an angel meet you?**

*A lot of angels, and a number of friends had met me on my entry into the spirit world.*

*I did not have a long list of deceased friends, but there were a few I had close friendships with, that had died before me.*

*In retrospect, I know that I, and they did not die – all we did is become lighter in our perspectives.*

*Lightness is the Mind of God.*

*I can hear in your mind – what was the role of the Wizard in Dorothy's dream?*

*In her dream of life, her mind kept searching for answers outside of herself.*

*All of life's answers are inside of each person – and it happens to be where God is, and answers them.*

## Thank you, Frank.
*I am always inside, giving answers as God. Nothing can be gained unless you ask.*

## Victor Fleming – Director

**Victor Fleming died of a heart attack, on the way to the hospital in Arizona, at the age of 59. May I speak with Victor?**
*I am Victor Fleming. How may I be of assistance in your consciousness research?*

**I am writing a book of messages from spirits of people involved in the 1939 making of *The Wizard of Oz* movie. What would you say is the theme of the movie?**
*I made it because I love its contrasting love and evil in its characters, and in having them all in Dorothy's mind. Nothing had been more important in the world at that time.*

**Those are really great points. It remains as one of the best movies ever made.**
*I am glad about it being a popular movie for each generation after its release.*

**You had a wonderful cast and crew.**
*I had a lot of help, meaning it is not my creation – although I did have my say in directing each scene.*

**You died at the relatively young age of 59, right after filming *Joan of Arc*.**
*I died because I had no more movies to make, that I could be proud of.*

**You could have retired, or trained others in movie-making.**
*Good point, but I also could have been defeated having no more creativity in myself, at my older age.*

*I can hear you asking if I think that is a true statement. It is not true, and I can tell you the truth.*

*I could have been more creative than ever, because I had a lot of experience in my craft. I could have hired a lot of the most talented people in the business also.*

*Life has its lessons, and mine was not giving in to fear and doubts.*

*How can I answer you if I am being asked another question?*

**Sorry.**
*I am hearing you ask if my lifetime had an ending date that had been planned in advance, or even before I came into my life. It had a long, or a wide range of time that could have been about 19 years longer, if I wanted it to be.*

**Did an angel meet you when you died, or ask you if you wanted to continue on living?**
*It did. How did you know to ask me that?*

**It is very common, or even standard for people to be given choices at the moment of death.**
*All I could have chosen was not to be in my dying body anymore. I could have gone back to before having a heart attack, and lived in a normal fashion, but I chose not to.*

**Did you prefer the feeling of total love and awareness, with no earthly concerns?**
*I did, and always will, in my eternal home.*

**Was the angel that met you your guardian angel?**
*It had been a guardian angel in my lifetime, and I hear you asking its name. It is 'Landin'.*

**Thank you, Victor.**
*I can add one more piece of information for you to write.*

*I am an aspect of God, within an aspect of myself, which is within an aspect of you and everyone else.*

**Where is that aspect within me?**
*It is in God's aspect, which is you – meaning it can only be in your mind, which lives forever.*

**Can we only access our God aspect with kind, loving, and generous thoughts?**
*Always–how can it be anything other than kind, loving, and generous thoughts?*

*It cannot – except for in nature which cannot be unkind, or unloving.*

**I teach people that having kind and loving thoughts – which exist only in the present moment – make us one with God Mind. When we are one with God Mind, there is no separation, and we can manifest our desires.**
*All correct, although God Mind has no desires – only you can have them.*

*In life, it gives you choices of what to desire – God, or all that is anti-God.*

*"Anti-God" is all non-loving thoughts in your mind.*

*I can hear in your mind – that is how Dorothy learned her life had been a dream.*

*She confronted her fears – and healed her mind, her heart, and her courage.*

**Thank you, Victor – for creating that timeless movie, which is a perfect metaphor for life.**

*And life after death – meaning how could death be real, if life is only a dream?*

## King Vidor – Director

King Vidor directed the last 3 weeks of primary filming, and the Kansas scenes for *The Wizard of Oz*. He died in 1982, at the age of 88.
The previous weekend, he and former lover Colleen Moore had driven up to San Simeon, William Randolph Hearst's 'Castle' to watch home movies made when they had been Hearst's guests there, 60 years before.
**May I speak with King?**
*About my having been in 'The Castle' – I had had a loving and committed relationship with Colleen in my younger years, but did not have relations with her after that. I can make the record straight.*

**That's fine.**
*I can also have it known how my directing in 'The Wizard of Oz' had been like making a film about how Dorothy allowed her imaginations, fears, and her dreams to become her reality.*

*In imagining how her life could be, in her 'Over the Rainbow' singing, her dream had its formation.*

*In it, her dream has Bluebirds that became a lot of Flying Monkeys – and they destroyed her heart, her mind, and her courage. How could her mind, her heart, and her courage be defeated by monkeys?*

*Her monkey attackers had known about her location, and her defenselessness against them.*

*Each monkey had been one of her fears, and all came from her one innermost fear of being separate from God. All she could do was have her mind, her heart, and her courage protect her, but they were not equipped to deal in fighting against wickedness. It was her dog that had been clever enough to help her.*

**What did her dog, Toto represent in her dream?**
*It had been her constant companion – and loyal to her, no matter how many others had been around.*

*It could have been her connection to her higher mind, which is her God-self – meaning her spirit, or soul's aspect of God.*

**That's an excellent answer. Thank you, King.**
*How did her dog appear in her lifetime dream? It escaped from a basket, and made her a vulnerable target for the evil witch. All she had to do to avoid her ordeal was to keep her mind, her heart, and her courage alert – so her dog, or God-self did not get away.*

**Awesome – you gave me a significant insight into one of the movie's lifetime metaphors.**
*I had directed the scenes where her dog is in Kansas with her.*

**The Kansas scenes are fantastic.**

*"How can it be a dark contrast to her dream?" had been my direction.*

**Let's talk about your lifetime dream. What was it like when you died?**

*I had died and awakened from my dream also. I was not awakened by my dog, or God-self. I had been awakened 'into' my God-self, by my God-self calling me home, like Dorothy being home again.*

*How I can describe it is if a person can be blasted high into the air, and the air is all love, and all awareness. It is an exhilaration that cannot be imagined.*

**Did an angel meet you then?**
*I had a lot of angels, and a number of friends and relatives meet me in my God-self home of all love and awareness. It is like Dorothy's home in the final scene, where her family had been all along – none of them having ever left, including Dorothy.*

**Thank you very much, King – and for your contributions to *The Wizard of Oz*.**
*It has been delightful, Mr. Gorman.*

## Billie Burke – Glinda

**Billie Burke played 'Glinda, the Good Witch of the North' in *The Wizard of Oz* movie. She died of Alzheimer's disease, at age 85 in Los Angeles, California, in 1970.**
**May I speak with Billie?**
*I am Billie Burke having a communication in my Light Mind, having no more life-mind, or body.*

*All I can hear is, am I alright having died from Alzheimer's? I died of old age. How could I have lived much longer?*

*It depends on what you call living – and if dying illuminates you in God, then how can it be called "death"?*

**Great points.**
*How can I be helpful in my illuminating God in my Light Mind? I am illuminating God in my Light Mind, which is illuminating in your Light Mind – which is illuminating in your life-mind, or left brain.*

*I hear your life-mind asking, how can I be better in illuminating information from my Light Mind, or right brain?*

*Begin by imagining a light in the middle of your brain. It is God, in a blue-magenta light that you know about.*[1]

*Allow it to increase in intensity in your mind. Alternate in having it illuminate each half of your brain, allowing each instance of illumination to heal the other half of the brain.*

*After alternating for about 10 minutes, the light illuminates both brain hemispheres.*

*All having both hemispheres illuminated will become God-like in their projections of their realities.*

**Wow – that is a great exercise, and complements what I know about God, the brain, and manifesting with light – all of which project our realities.**

*All in my communication here has been a lightness illuminating in part of your left brain, as it is allowed into your right brain.*

**Is there any way I can enhance that, other than with the alternating lightness exercise that you described?**

*Allow only lightness into all of your thoughts, and lightness is what heals all of your projections – allowing them to manifest in reality.*

**Thank you, Billie. Can you please tell me what happened when you died?**

---

[1] Discussed in *The Book of Manifesting*, 2024.

*As I was communicating to you, I did not die – I became alive in a moment of awakening, having no earthly attachments, allowing me to fly.*

*I hear in your mind asking – did an angel meet me in my God-like awareness, now that I had no body to hold me back?*

*I had a lot of angels, and also my friends and husband who had predeceased me.*

**What happened next?**
*I hovered over my deceased body for a while, and decided I did not need it any longer.*

**Did it seem like "a while" to you?**
*It could have been about 5 minutes, but I cannot measure in a timeline now.*

**Did you return to your soul groups?**
*I did, and I am always in my groups, having lessons instilled into my soul.*

**I almost forgot to ask you about *The Wizard of Oz* movie. What did 'Glinda, the Good Witch of the North' represent in Dorothy's mind?**
*Glinda healed Dorothy's fears by giving her life-mind its own powerful connection to God back.*

*God in the movie was all of the other characters healing in her mind – and having the evil character, meaning the bad witch, melt away into nothing but pure water. God is Dorothy healing in the moment she cared more about being home, than being in a dream trying to find help to get her there.*

**Wow – that's awesome. I never knew where God was in the movie. I think Glinda was her higher-self, and the little people were her thoughts – all convinced that she was lost.**

*I agree, and all of the little people had hope for Dorothy to get home.*

**Thank you, Billie. Would you like to add anything else?**

*In life, heal all that is fearful because it is an illusion that is only in your dream for you to heal it.*

## CHARLEY GRAPEWIN – UNCLE HENRY

Charley Grapewin played Dorothy's 'Uncle Henry' in *The Wizard of Oz* movie. He died of natural causes in 1956, at home in California, at the age of 86.

**May I speak with Charley?**
*All I can hear is how did Uncle Henry fit into Dorothy's dream of a life?*

*I had been a guiding force in her life, because her parents didn't appear, did they?*

**That's a great point – I never noticed they were missing. How could her parents have fit into her dream of a life?**
*Her parental figures were myself and Aunt Em – plus a few farmhands, having befriended her in the movie.*

**Thank you, Charley. You had an impressive acting career, having been in over 100 films. You were also a Vaudeville and circus performer, a writer, and a stage actor.**
*All I ever had an interest in was acting – not in films necessarily, but acting on a stage.*

**Can you tell me what it was like when you died?**
*In my life, I had never thought about death, although it had been all around me.*

*Dying had been a lot like Dorothy going home – but imagine it having only love, all awareness, no fear –*

*and death is not even a concept, other than awakening in God.*

*How could death even exist, if life had been a dream of having been separated from God?*

**That's a great point. Did angels meet you when you died?**
*I had one angel meet me in my awakening into all awareness. It had been my angel and guardian in life. It asked me if I knew my life was ending. I answered it in the affirmative, because how else could I have met an angel?*

*I could have, but did not know how I could have, in my lifetime dream.*

**How can we meet angels in our lifetime dreams?**
*All you have to do is ask your angel to heal all in your mind that needs healing, and it will heal it in God's love – although you have to ask for its help, and allow its healing. A healed mind is higher in consciousness, and can see angels.*

**Did you proceed away from the Earth with your angel?**
*I could have, but I was awakened from my dream of Earth living.*

**Thank you, Charley.**
*You are healing in your dream, as one who has an interest in awakening from a dream – while still being in it.*

## CLARA BLANDICK – AUNTIE EM

**Clara Blandick played Dorothy's 'Aunt Em', in *The Wizard of Oz* movie. She died of suicide in 1962, at the age of 85.**
**May I speak with Clara?**
*I am Clara. Hello, Mr. Gorman. I expected I would be in your book of healing messages, since I had been Dorothy's 'Aunt Em' in The Wizard of Oz movie.*

**Hello, Clara. I was surprised to learn that you took your own life. It was reported that you dressed immaculately, then took an overdose of sleeping pills. You had left a note that read, "I am now about to make the great adventure. I cannot endure this agonizing pain any longer. It is all over my body. Neither can I face the impending blindness. I pray the Lord my soul to take. Amen."**
**Your ashes are interred just yards away from our last guest, Charley Grapewin.**
*I died in my sleep, and I awakened in heaven. I could have lived a little longer, but I had no desire to.*

**Was it like when Dorothy awakened from her dream of a life?**
*I had always wondered what it would be like when I died, and I didn't expect for my death to be as exhilarating as it had been, and still is. I felt like I had been in an airtight container, unable to breathe – and*

*then I exited it into an atmosphere of fresh air and sunshine, having no container at all.*

**It was way better than Dorothy's awakening in the closing movie scene.**
*I agree, but Dorothy's closing scene had her surrounded by love – that is accurate.*

**Thank you, Clara. What else would you like to add?**
*I had been an actress in my life, but now I am not acting at all. I am an all-aware aspect of God, that has no need to act. I only have healing desires, much like in life – but I am aware of it now.*

*I hear you asking – what caused my arthritis, and losing my eyesight?*

*I had a lot of heartache in my divorce, and in my life after my divorce. All I had in my life for companionship were my acting companions.*

**Would you like to add any advice for people?**
*Acting has its advantages, if you are acting in a dream, knowing it is only an act. The advantage of acting is knowing that it is only an image you are projecting.*

*In God Mind, there is no image – only an imaginary dream, having images to heal.*

**Thank you, Clara.**
*I am appreciative of your including me in your book of messages from our acting cast, and production crew.*

## Pat Walshe – Nikko

Pat Walshe played 'Nikko', leader of the Winged Monkeys in *The Wizard of Oz* movie, because of his animal impersonating skills. He died of a heart attack in Los Angeles, in 1991, at age 91. He was the last surviving cast member of *The Wizard of Oz*. May I speak with Pat?

*How can I help you in writing about how I had been a Flying Monkey in the movie?*

*I had a lot of good luck in my life, especially in that role. I gave it all I could in acting how a monkey acts.*

*All I can hear you asking is if I had a lot of work in preparing for that role. I could act like a monkey, but I had to 'be' a monkey for that role. To 'be' a monkey, I had to live like a monkey for a few months before filming began. I would go to hear and watch the monkeys in a zoo, as much as I could – and it gave me a lot of insight on how they would react to each other. I memorized all of the inflections in their movements, and in their having nothing but animal minds. I became like a monkey in my mind, when I was alone.*

**It was hard to believe that it wasn't a monkey in the movie.**
*I gave it all I had, as I said.*

**This is a book about our journeys out of this life. Can you tell me what it was like when you died?**

*I can describe it – and describing it is not going to be as incredible as it is – but I became a light being.*

*My body became insignificant, and unnecessary. It had been my animal costume – for imitating animals, if that makes any sense. All I could have hoped for in life had been accomplished, and my life had been completed in my dream of it.*

### What did the Winged Monkeys represent in Dorothy's mind?
*All of her ego demands, and ego judgments of herself that debilitated her mind, her heart, and her courage.*

*Her heart, her mind, and her courage – along with her dog – helped her to defeat the entire kingdom of the Wicked Witch.*

### Is it because she was an aspect of God, and the Land of Oz in her dream was an illusion?
*I can agree with it, now having a God insight into what you are writing.*

### Thank you, Pat. Would you like to add anything else?
*In life, it is not necessary to have incidents of healing your mind, heart, and courage – they are all that you are. You only have to overcome the ego demands that hide them.*

## L. Frank Baum – Author

Author L. Frank Baum had a stroke, slipped into a coma, and died the following day, at the age of 62. It was in 1919, nine days before his 63rd birthday – and 20 years before *The Wizard of Oz* movie was made. He wrote 'The Wonderful Wizard of Oz' in 1900, and a series of 13 more 'Oz' books, that were published up until 1920.

**May I speak with Frank?**
*"All I can believe, is all I can become." That had been my belief in life.*

*I am hearing – how did I have a stroke, at only 62? I could have lived a little bit longer, but I had made an agreement before I was born, to leave before my 63rd birthday.*

**Why did you pick that particular age limit for your life?**
*All I could have done had nothing to do with my age. Age is an agreement, like everything else.*

*It is an artificial construction, having nothing in it that is meaningful, other than what you give it.*

*I decided I could complete my goals in that amount of life – meaning I could heal my mind in that amount of time.*

**I do not know if *The Wizard of Oz* movie is true to your book themes.**
*It has a lot of analogous interpretations, but I did not have it ending the way that it did.*

**Can you please tell me about your lifetime ending?**
*An angel came into my head, and it gave me another option for living in my debilitated condition, or to continue on as I had already agreed. I did not have an interest in continuing on in my debilitated condition, meaning I had accepted that I was going to die, and continue on with the angel.*

**What did you feel?**
*I felt an all-encompassing love, that I cannot begin to express in words.*

*I can hear in your mind, asking how I am doing, now that I'm dead. I'm doing all that I ever dreamed I could do, making my death the most loving, and healing experience I could ever have hoped for.*

*It is a little bit tricky because I manifest everything I think of, even if it is not for my healing – much like in life, but in life there is a lag time. Manifesting in life allows a person his or her own desires a birth in life, or not.*

*How can it be healing if it is any other way?*

*All I can hear in your mind is – how is life like the movie of my books? I am hearing in your mind that the movie was made long after I had died. I can access any information in my advanced awareness.*

*I loved a lot in the movie, except for the apple orchard scene. Apples are not evil like the Adam and Eve story.*

*In an evil apple orchard, they would not have wanted the apples from the tree.*

*Having the apples would have made them highly incapable of defeating the evil witch.*

**That's a really great point.**
*It cannot be deleted now.*

**Thank you for your input, Frank. Is there anything else you would like to say to the readers of this book, that is being written in 2025?**
*"All I can believe, is all I can become" – in a lifetime dream, or in an afterlife awakened.*

*Having it in both is all you can ever be. Believe in your ability as God, to be all that your heart desires.*

*Allow your heart, your mind, and your courage to guide you.*

## Appendix
## Biographies

**Terry**, the female Cairn Terrier who played Toto, was a trained animal actor owned by Carl Spitz and was paid $125 per week, more than the Munchkin actors.

**Judy Garland** began performing at age 2 and, despite immense professional success, faced lifelong struggles with studio-mandated diet pills, sleep aids, and self-esteem.

**Margaret Hamilton**, a former kindergarten teacher, became typecast as a villain but was a dedicated advocate for children and education who often softened her witch persona for young fans.

**Ray Bolger** was a classically trained dancer who achieved his greatest fame in vaudeville and on Broadway, where his role in *Where's Charley?* earned him a Tony Award.

**Jack Haley**, a vaudeville and Broadway performer, nearly lost his eyesight from the aluminum powder makeup used for the Tin Man, an allergy that forced a change to an aluminum paste.

**Bert Lahr** was a major star of burlesque and Broadway, celebrated for his comic persona, and his performance in the play *Waiting for Godot* late in his career earned critical acclaim.

**Frank Morgan**, born Francis Wuppermann, came from a wealthy family (his father owned the company that made Angostura bitters) and enjoyed a prolific four-decade film career.

**Victor Fleming** was a former race car driver and cinematographer who was MGM's most trusted director for difficult productions, helming both *The Wizard of Oz* and *Gone with the Wind* in 1939.

**King Vidor**, a respected and innovative director nominated for five Academy Awards, was brought in to direct the Kansas sequences during a production hiatus.

**Billie Burke**, a famous Broadway actress, married impresario Florenz Ziegfeld, Jr., and successfully transitioned to film, often playing flighty, charming matrons to support their lifestyle after his financial losses.

**Charley Grapewin** was a veteran character actor whose career spanned from silent films to the 1940s, famously playing Grandpa Joad in *The Grapes of Wrath* after his role as Uncle Henry.

**Clara Blandick** was a stage and film actress for over four decades who took her own life in 1962 at age 81, citing failing health as the reason in her suicide note.

**Pat Walshe** was a little-person actor and former circus performer who appeared in numerous films, often in animalistic roles, and was known for his skill in pantomime.

**L. Frank Baum** was a prolific author, playwright, and sometime businessman whose series of 14 Oz books became a classic of American children's literature.

## Directors and Writers

**Directors**
Victor Fleming
George Cukor – intermediary (uncredited)
Norman Taurog – test scenes (uncredited)
Richard Thorpe – initial shoot (uncredited)
King Vidor – Kansas scenes

**Writers**
Noel Langley – screenplay
Florence Ryerson – screenplay
Edgar Allen Woolf – screenplay
Noel Langley – adaptation
Irving Brecher – contributing writer
William H Cannon – (uncredited)
George Cukor – contributing writer (uncredited)
Herbet Fields – contributing writer (uncredited)
Arthur Freed – contributing writer (uncredited)
L. Frank Baum – author
Jack Haley – additional dialogue (uncredited)
E.Y. Harburg – contributing writer (uncredited)
Samuel Hoffenstein – contributing writer (uncredited)
Bert Lahr – additional dialogue (uncredited)
John Lee Mahin – contributing writer (uncredited)
Herman J. Mankiewicz – contributing writer (uncredited)
Jack Mintz – contributing writer (uncredited)
Ogden Nash – contributing writer (uncredited)

Robert Pirosh – contributing writer (uncredited)
George Seaton – contributing writer (uncredited)
Sid Silvers – contributing writer (uncredited)
Richard Thorpe – contributing writer (uncredited)
King Vidor – contributing writer (uncredited)

## ABOUT THE AUTHOR

From God Mind:

*Paul Gorman illuminates as a spiritual researcher,
writing his discoveries into books,
allowing healing in the minds
of all who read them.*